My Hometown Heroes

FIREFIGHTERS to the rescue!

(Fire Safety For Kids)

Illustrated by:
Iona Cordero and Stevan Mitric

Rev. date 09/01/2016
Published by Magicwonders4kidz

To order additional copies of this book visit:

www.ionacordero.com

www.amazon.com

www.barnes&noble.com

Dedication

Special Thanks to
Fire Chief Rafael Balderas
David J. Spencer and Alfred Pena
for the inspiration of this book

I.C.

We will begin with what is a FIREFIGHTER?

A FIREFIGHTER

-

IS A PERSON WHO FIGHTS FIRES AND RESCUES PEOPLE AND ANIMALS FROM FIRE...

Firefighters don't dress like you and me. They wear protective gear and clothing that will keep them safe from fires.

WHAT CAN FIREFIGHTERS DO FOR YOU ?

HERE ARE JUST A FEW EXAMPLES OF

HOW THEY CAN HELP TAKE CARE OF YOU

AND YOUR FAMILY IN CASE OF AN EMERGENCY

Playing

With

Fire

Some of your friends may tell you that playing with fire is ok...But its Not!
In this picture you can see kids playing with fire because they think it is fun and exciting, but playing with fire is very dangerous and can have serious consequences.

Things can change very quickly when playing with fire. Just like the boy in this picture, his shirt catches fire burning straight through causing pain and burning to his arm.
What you should do?
Stop drop and roll and call 911.

Firefighters can also help take care of your wounds till more help arrives.
Playing with fire can leave pain and scars to last you for days, weeks or months.
So stand tall and be proud to just say no to playing with fire.

HERE ARE SOME DO'S AND DONT'S

YOU SHOULD KNOW IN CASE OF A HOUSE FIRE.

House

Fire

These are a few things that can cause fires in your house

Candles

Stove

Lighter

Matches

Heater

Lint Filter

Dryer

overloaded wall sockets

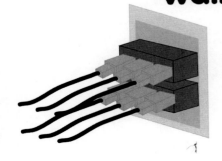

Cigarette

IT IS VERY IMPORTANT TO HAVE AN ESCAPE PLAN READY.

KNOW ALL YOUR EXITS AT ALL TIMES .

Escape Plan

Back Door

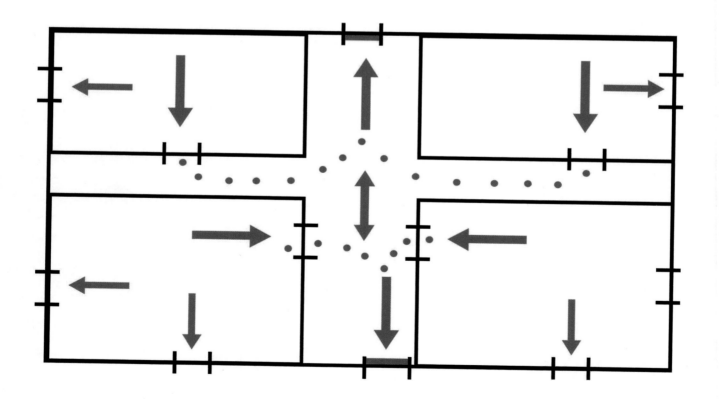

Front Door

One common item that can cause a house fire
in your home is (candles).
Leaving candles lit overnight or by a curtain can
cause a house fire just like this...

If you find yourself in bed
when a fire occurs
do not sit up in bed. The smoke can harm
your lungs and make it hard for you to breath.

The correct way is to roll off the side of your bed staying clear of the smoke.

Do not go underneath your bed or to your closet. This will make it harder and longer for the fire-fighters to find you and take you to safety.

The correct thing to do is roll off your bed and remember your escape plan. But should you find yourself trapped in your room go to nearest wall and wait for the firefighters to find you.

You will hear loud noises and yelling where the firefighters will be going into your home calling out to look for you. Do not worry they are going to find you and save you.

Because the house will be full of smoke
the firefighters can not see, so they will follow the
walls through out the house

going room by room till they find you and take you to safety.

Once the firefighters have taken you outside to safety, stay far away from the house and close to your parents. In this picture you can see Michael the little boy running back to the burning house, he does not see his sister and thinks she's still inside.

Michael steps inside and drops to the floor, he can't see or breath. There's too much smoke and fire everywhere. Now he needs help.

As you can see Michael sister was able to follow the escape plane and run out the back door.

She is now safe with the firefighters.

Michael was rescued and happy to see his sister safe, but almost lost his life thinking she was inside. If you see someone in your family missing do not run back inside to find them. Stay outside at all times and let the firefighters do what they do best stop fires and save lives.

WITH OUR PARENTS DRIVING US TO SCHOOL
ITS VERY IMPORTANT FOR ALL OF US TO WORK TOGEHTER
IN KEEPING OUR FAMILY SAFE
WHILE BEING IN A MOVING VEHICLE.

Car

Accident

HOW CAN YOU HELP?
YOU CAN HELP BY UNDERSTANDING WHAT KIND OF THINGS
YOU SHOULD NOT DO IN A MOVING CAR.
HERE ARE A FEW THINGS THAT CAN
CAUSE A CAR ACCIDENT WHILE ON THE ROAD

CELL PHONE DRINKING AND DRIVING* CAR DISTRACTION*

Firefighters can help you during a car accident
when you are hurt.

Firefighters use very special tools to help get you out of the car safely.These tools can be loud and sometimes scary, but remember firefighters are there to help you.

Firefighters will check if you have any cuts, bruises or broken bones.
You must tell the firefighter exactly where you are hurting so they can take care of you till more help arrives.

So if you were sitting in the front seat, or forgot to put on your seat belt, you must always tell the truth.

Firefighters are not there to get mad at you or get you in trouble. They are only there to take care of you and get you all the help you need to be safe.

Firefighters

are

People like

You and Me

Fire Station

You have your home and this is their home.

They have lunch just like you and me.

They fall to sleep just like you and me.

They have their closets just slightly different then
yours and mine.
Although many things seem just the same,
firefighters lives can be very different to.

They have to be ready to go stop a fire or help someone in trouble day or night.
The fire alarm rings and their day begins even when they are having dinner they must get up and go.

When they are sleeping in the middle of the night and the fire alarm rings, they must wake up and GO GO GO !

Firefighters dedicate themselves everyday to doing what they do best, stop fires and save lives. Giving us a much more safer place to live.

The End

Made in the USA
Columbia, SC
12 September 2019